WITHDRAWN

Measuring Price Changes:

a study of the price indexes

———◆———

by
William H. Wallace

FEDERAL RESERVE BANK OF RICHMOND
DECEMBER, 1970

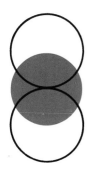

Contents

3

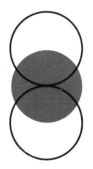

Introduction

For the past five years, the dominant economic problem in the United States has been inflation. The accelerating intensity of this problem has brought increased attention to the indexes which are rough measures of its magnitude. Informed discussion of inflation and of policies directed at its control are predicated on the assumption that some reliable and appropriate means exists to measure changes in the general level of prices over time. Analysts and policymakers have thus watched every movement, however minute, of the major indexes for some indication of progress in the effort to bring inflation under control. Considerable importance is therefore placed upon the indexes in the determination of policy and in the evaluation of the effectiveness of policy.

This three-part article is an examination of price indexes. The first part contains a discussion of the recent behavior of prices as measured by the major indexes. It serves the preliminary purpose of setting the stage for a discussion of the indexes themselves by emphasizing the severity of the current inflation problem and illustrating the importance of a good measure of price changes. The second part is expository in nature. Its purpose is to explain the meaning of a price index, to review the criteria which a good price index must meet, and to discuss the conceptual and statistical problems associated with the design and construction of price indexes. The final part is an analysis and criticism of the major price indexes in current use in the United States—the Consumer Price Index, the Wholesale Price Index, and the GNP Implicit Price Deflator. An examination of the methodologies used in the major indexes is presented in the light of the criteria discussed in the second part in order to reveal the limitations as well as the appropriate interpretations of the indexes.

A short list of references is presented at the end of the article to aid the reader interested in pursuing more detailed research on price indexes.[1]

---

[1] This article first appeared as a three-part series in the Federal Reserve Bank of Richmond's *Monthly Review*, the September, October, and November, 1970 issues.

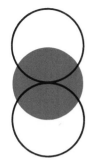

Recent
Price Behavior

Inflation was recently characterized by the Commissioner of Labor Statistics as a rise in prices which is both general and widely diffused [16, p. 3]. Accompanying charts of the indexes indicate the generality of the price increases which have occurred in this country in recent years. They also show the acceleration which has taken place in the price rises in nearly all categories since about 1965. That year is most commonly thought of as the beginning of the current period of serious inflation.

It should be noted that this article is concerned not with the question of inflation specifically but with that of prices and price indexes. While price increases are symptomatic of inflation, a thorough analysis of the subject of inflation must cover a wide range of complex topics, including both demand and cost pressures and their interaction, monetary and fiscal policy, productivity factors, and the consequences of inflation, including its differential impact on various groups. Thus, the questions to be considered in this article are limited to how much price increase there has been, and how it is measured.

The charts show annual figures for the indexes on a ratio scale which permits visual comparisons of percentage rates of change. The average annual rates of change in the indexes are shown as straight lines on the ratio scale. These average rates are given for the entire period, 1960 through 1970, and for the recent period, 1965 through 1970. No attempt is made in this first part to comment upon the merits of the particular indexes under discussion. Attention is focused upon the implications of the movements in the indexes.

The figures shown on the charts are the published annual averages of the indexes except those for 1970, which are estimated from the figures published for the first three quarters of the year. The average annual rates of growth are based upon these averages. In comparing price changes which occur in a given year with those which occurred in the preceding year, it is often more meaningful to compare year-end to year-end changes. In a period of rapidly accelerating prices, the result could differ significantly between the two approaches, with the comparison of annual averages understating the true increase. But, in comparing price changes over a longer span of time, the difference is of less importance. It is likely, therefore, that growth rates shown for the 1965 through 1970 period are slightly lower than they would have been if year-end indexes had been used. One of the principal objectives of the charts, however, is to show the speed-up of price increases in the latter half of the decade, and that point is clearly illustrated with annual average indexes.

Consumer Prices

Chart I shows values of the Consumer Price Index for all items and for the major categories, all commodities, food, and services. The chart shows a relatively modest increase in prices of consumer items over the first half of the decade, with services increasing at a faster pace than either of the other categories or the total.

The prices of all categories of consumer items began to increase more rapidly in 1965, with services again outpacing the other groups. This rapid advance in the services category reflects the pressure of demand resulting from the growing importance of services in the consumer's budget.

Figures for 1970, estimated from the results of the first three quarters, indicate that the rates of advance in the all-items and all-commodities groups have tapered somewhat from the 1969 pace. The food and services categories show some further acceleration in 1970 over 1969. An analysis of within-year changes based on quarterly figures, however, reveals some progressive softening in the rates of advance during 1970 for all items and the three major categories.

The Consumer Price Index is available in more detail than that shown in the charts. A further breakdown indicates that the rate of increase for the 1965 to 1970 period has been more pronounced in prices of nondurable items than in prices of durable consumer goods. This is true even if food, which has in-

Chart I
INDEXES OF CONSUMER PRICES
1957-1959 = 100

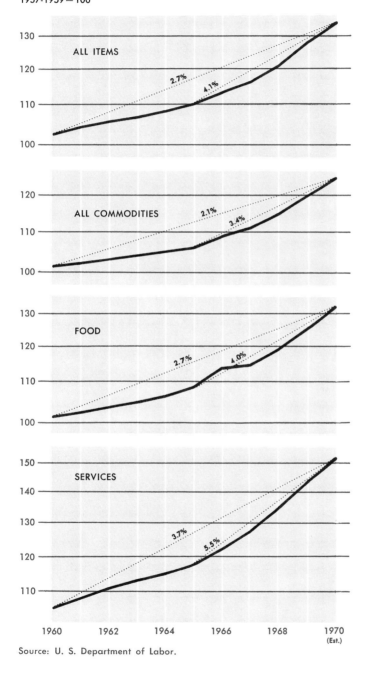

Source: U. S. Department of Labor.

9

creased more than other nondurables, is excluded from the non-durable group. Increases have been relatively moderate in the durable consumer goods category. Prices of consumer services have been boosted substantially by increases in costs of medical care, public transportation, and numerous costs associated with home ownership, such as mortgage rates, repair services, etc. These sub-groups present a somewhat more complete picture of the current consumer price problem although they are still relatively broad in scope. A fully detailed discussion of movements in the 400 items comprising the Consumer Price Index is beyond the purpose of this article.

A geographic breakdown of the Consumer Price Index is also available. Some details of the geographic sampling procedures are discussed in the final part, but it is useful here to compare the indexes for certain locations with the U. S. average. For example, prices of all consumer items have risen more than the national average in Boston, New York, Philadelphia, Minneapolis-St. Paul, Washington, Kansas City, and San Francisco-Oakland. Numerous other cities for which the index is published are below the national average. There are 23 Standard Metropolitan Statistical Areas for which indexes are published as well as 33 other cities, some of which are SMSA's, from which samples are taken for use in deriving the national indexes. While indexes for SMSA's cannot be used to compare costs of living among geographic areas directly, the recent movements of these indexes indicate that inflation has not exempted any area of the country. Indexes for all areas exhibit the kind of rapid price increase that has been typical of the U. S. at large for the last several years though there are significant differences among some of the cities in the rate of advance.

Wholesale Prices

Chart II shows the Wholesale Price Index for all commodities and industrial commodities, and the Index of 22 Basic Commodities which the Bureau of Labor Statistics classifies as among the most sensitive to changes in economic conditions. Movements in the Wholesale Price Index, which presently includes over 2,300 items, are generally believed to portend changes in prices of consumer goods, though the index differs considerably

Chart II

INDEXES OF WHOLESALE PRICES
1957-1959 = 100

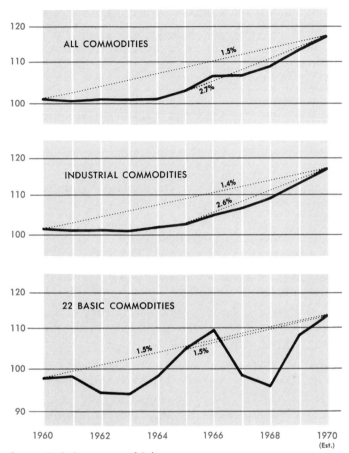

Source: U. S. Department of Labor.

in design and coverage from the Consumer Price Index. Therefore, this index is one of those indicators most closely watched for evidence of progress in the effort to halt inflation.

Like consumer goods prices, wholesale prices were relatively stable during the first half of the decade of the 1960's, but began to advance rapidly in about 1965. Chart II indicates that this was true of all commodities and industrial commodities. Tentative 1970 figures, however, indicate some tapering of the rates of growth of prices of all commodities and of industrial commodities from 1969.

11

Certain components of the Wholesale Price Index have historically tended to move quite erratically. This is particularly true of farm products where changes in supply conditions can affect prices significantly within relatively short time periods. Farm products prices, for example, averaged below their base period (1957 to 1959) levels throughout the 1960's, except for 1966, 1968, and 1969. The one category of items, aside from industrial commodities, which has caused the all-commodities index to accelerate rapidly in recent years is processed foods and feeds, where increasing costs at the several stages of processing are reflected. Within this group, price increases on dairy products, processed fruits and vegetables, and cereals and bakery products have been the largest.

The industrial commodities component of the Wholesale Price Index has risen steadily since 1964, following a three-year period of practically no change. The overall rise in this component has been paced by increases in such categories as lumber, machinery and equipment, leather products, metals, and minerals, while other important categories such as textiles, chemicals, fuels, and appliances have advanced with relative moderation. Of course, there are exceptions in both directions within each of these sub-categories, such as paint, in the chemicals group, which has advanced substantially, and electrical equipment, within the machinery and equipment group, which has risen in price only moderately. In other words, the incidence of the increase is obscured by looking only at the aggregative indexes. There are some questions concerning the sensitivity of the Wholesale Price Index to changes in prices which will be discussed in the final part.

Initial inspection of the 22 basic commodities chart reveals a somewhat confused picture. This group consists of 9 foodstuffs and 13 raw industrial commodities for which there are daily spot market prices on organized exchanges. The basic concept underlying this index emphasizes that the commodities included in it are close to the initial production stage so that their prices do not include the labor and capital costs or profit margins added in later stages of processing. Accordingly, price changes in these commodities should reflect fundamental changes in supply and demand conditions in given markets and should be among the earliest indications of changes that may be reflected later in the Wholesale Price Index and ultimately, in the Consumer Price Index [3, p. 43]. Thus, while this index is not a part of the Wholesale Price Index, many of the items included in it are picked up at more advanced stages of production in the Wholesale Price Index.

While the average annual growth over the long period, 1960 through 1970, in the 22 basic commodities is positive and matches the growth of all commodities, Chart II shows that the pattern of the increases since 1965 differs markedly between the two groups. Instead of one continuous period of rapid increase which characterizes the other categories of more highly processed items, this chart reveals that there have been two periods of rapid increase—from 1963 through 1966 and again from 1968 to 1970. It might be argued that the earlier period foretold the inflation which was to follow in the 1965 to 1970 period as the increased labor and capital costs were added to the rising prices of the basic commodities. The latter period of increase should be reflected in wholesale and consumer prices currently. An encouraging sign is the tapering of the rate of growth in the prices of the basic commodities which began in 1970. Recently, outright declines have occurred in several of the basic commodity prices.

GNP Deflator

Chart III shows the aggregate deflator for gross national product. Each component of GNP, in as fine detail as possible, is deflated for a given year or quarter by the indexes which are appropriate for the particular component. Once deflated, the components are again aggregated to obtain GNP in constant dollars, and the aggregate GNP deflator is found by dividing current dollar GNP by constant dollar GNP. Thus, the deflator is an implicit index derived in a roundabout manner.

Since the index depends upon previously determined indexes of consumer and wholesale prices, as well as several other indexes, its direct interpretation has some definite limitations. For example, sub-components of the consumer spending component of GNP are deflated by the appropriate indexes which comprise the Consumer Price Index and, where applicable, by the index of prices paid by farmers which is compiled by the

13

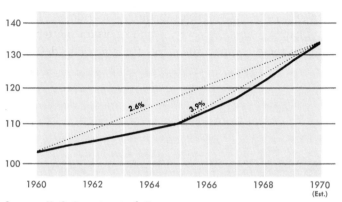

Chart III
GNP DEFLATOR
1958=100

140

130

120

110

100

1960   1962   1964   1966   1968   1970
(Est.)

Source: U. S. Department of Commerce.

U. S. Department of Agriculture. The gross private domestic investment component of GNP is deflated by various component indexes of the Wholesale Price Index. Construction, in the investment component of GNP, is deflated by construction cost indexes prepared by the Bureau of the Census. Deflation of the government spending component of GNP depends on all of the above indexes. Thus, the resulting aggregate GNP Deflator is a mixture of the effects of these several indexes, and its value for any given period depends upon the composition of GNP for that period as between business, government, and consumer spending, and in turn, the particular composition of spending within each of these categories [9]. Further discussion of the technical qualities of the GNP Deflator is contained in the final part.

Chart III shows that the "price" of the gross national product has advanced consistently over the long period, 1960 through 1970, but increased in pace as the other price indexes did in 1965. Again, however, the estimated 1970 figure indicates some tapering of the rate of increase in 1970, in comparison to 1969. A further breakdown reveals that certain components have advanced more rapidly since 1965 than the aggregate deflator— the services component of consumer spending, the residential and nonresidential construction components of investment spending, and state and local government spending. Until 1969, the federal spending component was substantially below the aggre-

14

gate deflator in its rate of advance. Also, the producers' durable equipment and consumer durable goods components rose more slowly than the aggregate. These results reflect what was said earlier about prices of durables in the other indexes. The distribution of expenditures, however, is an important matter in determining how these components affect the aggregate deflator.

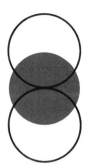

The Design
and Construction
of Price Indexes

An index in the simplest sense is a ratio of one quantity to another. It expresses a given quantity in terms of its relative value in comparison to a base quantity. Thus, a price index designed for the purpose of measuring price changes over time is a ratio of one price (or combination of prices) to the price of the same item (or combination of items) in a different period of time. When properly constructed, index numbers of prices permit the comparison of economic values over time net of the effect of price changes.

Several conceptual and statistical issues involved in the development of meaningful and reliable price indexes to represent the aggregate movement of prices over time are raised in the discussion which follows.

For purposes of illustration of the concepts, a hypothetical example is used throughout the discussion of a consumer whose total budget consists of five items, and whose expenditures on the items are shown for a period of four years. Three of the items are large in relation to his total budget—automobiles and suits, which are purchased infrequently, and rent, which is paid frequently. Two of the items are small, but one, bread, is purchased frequently, and the other, movie tickets, is purchased infrequently. The five items taken together comprise a theoretical "market basket"—a term commonly used to refer to the sample of items upon which an index is based. Usually, the "market basket" is a sample of selected items typical of the consumer's purchases and is used to represent his total budget. In this simplified example, however, it is assumed that the five items comprise this consumer's total budget. Table I shows the consumer's situation. This example, though an over simplification of the problems involved in constructing aggregate price indexes, illustrates a number of the issues.

16

Conceptual Problems

THE BASE PERIOD   A fundamental problem in the development of index numbers is the selection of a base. If a price index is to serve as a stable basis for comparison of price movements over time, a period of time must be selected and held as the base long enough to generate a series of indexes for subsequent periods that will be useful in comparing those periods not only with the base, but with each other. Price indexes designed for analysis of price changes over time which are also computed for different places, such as the Consumer Price Index, do not automatically provide a valid basis of comparison of one place with another. Since the index relates current prices at a particular location to those in the base period at the same location, without regard to the standardization of base prices among the several locations, the index is useful only for comparisons over time. Current usage of price indexes is generally restricted to temporal comparisons. Therefore, attention is devoted only to indexes designed for that purpose in the discussion which follows.

Where the object is to devise an aggregate index for general-purpose use, the selection of a base period is necessarily somewhat arbitrary. Under ideal conditions, however, the base period would be one in which extremely erratic movements are not occurring in prices themselves or in underlying economic conditions which would be reflected in prices. Such "normal" periods are difficult to define where prices of hundreds of items must be taken into account. Where the index is more of the special-purpose variety, the selection of an appropriate base is somewhat easier. For example, the earliest concern with index numbers involved an attempt to measure the change in the purchasing power of money (i.e., the reciprocal of the price index) resulting from the importation of silver into Europe after the discovery of America. This first price index, developed by Carli in 1764, covered a 250 year time span with the year 1500 as the base [17, p. 6].

Base periods of price indexes are occasionally updated for convenience. As spending patterns change and as technological change occurs, particular selections of goods and services comprising the "market basket" become obsolete as standards for comparison. Items which are commonly purchased in a current

17

period may not have been available in the base period or may have undergone substantial technical or quality changes since the base period. This requires a revision of the sample, and this change may be accompanied by a shift of the base period to a later one for which the revised sample of goods and services is representative.

Though it is sometimes desirable, it is not necessary that both of the above changes be made at the same time. An updating of the sample of goods and services can be accomplished without shifting the base if the revised selection of items is worked into the sample so as not to distort the continuity of the index. This type of adjustment is discussed later in connection with other statistical problems. A straightforward shift of the base period is possible, however, without changing the sample of goods and services if it is known that the original sample selection remains valid, and if all that is desired is a revision of the index base to a more recent date. For example, if the index of 1970 prices for a particular sample of items on a 1960 base is 120.0, and the index on the same base was 105.0 in 1965, then 1970 prices can be expressed on a 1965 base as 114.3, or $120.0/105.0$[2] This kind of linkage, while frequently used, does nothing to improve the quality of the index. The revised number gives the same information that the original index did, but expresses it in terms of a more recent base. The revision in no way allows for changes in quality of goods and services or changes in spending patterns which result from price changes. Thus, the crucial question to which an index must frequently be subjected is whether or not the sample of commodities is currently valid. If it is, no revisions of the base period or the sample are needed. On the other hand, if revisions of the sample are needed, a shift of the base period may be convenient, but not essential.

SIMPLE AVERAGE OF RELATIVES AND SIMPLE AGGREGATIVE PRICE INDEXES
The simplest form of price index is the ratio of one price to another for a specified commodity. This approach is valid under extremely restricted

[2] It is common practice to express index numbers as ratios multiplied by 100 and rounded to one decimal place (e.g., the index 114.3 is the ratio 1.143). It is understood throughout this article that a ratio obtained by any formula is multiplied by 100 to obtain an index. For simplicity that step is not shown in the calculations or formulas.

Table I

HYPOTHETICAL CONSUMER WITH A FIVE-ITEM "MARKET BASKET"

Prices and Quantities Purchased

Item	Years							
	1		2		3		4	
	p_1	q_1	p_2	q_2	p_3	q_3	p_4	q_4
Automobiles, each	$2,000.00	1	$2,200.00	1	$2,500.00	0	$2,500.00	1
Rent, per month	$ 80.00	12	$ 85.00	12	$ 100.00	12	$ 130.00	12
Bread, per loaf	$ .20	250	$ .22	275	$ .25	275	$ .23	300
Movie tickets, each	$ .75	10	$ 1.00	6	$ 1.25	10	$ 1.35	10
Suits, each	$ 85.00	4	$ 95.00	4	$ 115.00	3	$ 135.00	1
Total Expenditures	$3,357.50		$3,666.50		$1,626.25		$4,277.50	

Note: Subscripts represent years, and p and q represent prices and quantities respectively.

circumstances. For example, consider the consumer whose expenditures are shown in Table I. Assuming that the loaf of bread listed in the table is the same loaf in size and quality in all four years, a simple index of the price of bread in year 2 is 110.0 (year 1 = 100). For years 3 and 4, the index is 125.0 and 115.0, respectively. As far as it goes, this index is a valid measure of changes in the price of bread.

If no change in quality could be assumed for the other four items shown, similar price indexes could be constructed for them. But a serious problem arises, even in the absence of any quality changes, if a composite index of this consumer's "market basket" is desired. Consider, for example, only the change between years 1 and 2. The price index for bread, as previously stated, is 110.0; for automobiles, it is also 110.0; for rent, it is 106.3; for movie tickets, it is 133.3; and for suits, it is 111.8. A simple average of the individual indexes yields a composite index of 114.3 for this consumer's total budget in year 2, based upon year 1. This index is questionable since it implicitly gives the highest weight among the five items to that one which rises most in price in percentage terms. That item is movie tickets, one which is of relatively little consequence to this consumer.

The index formula used in the above illustration is known as a simple average of relatives, or

$$I_{1\,2} = \Sigma(p_2/p_1)/n,$$

where $I_{1\,2}$ represents the value of the index for year 2 based upon year 1; p_1 and p_2 represent prices of individual items in years 1 and 2, respectively; Σ is the standard symbol for summation; and n is the number of items comprising the index [15, Ch. 13].

Other means of averaging the price relatives (or ratios) could easily be used. For example, a median of relatives (110.0 in this case) reduces the upward bias resulting from the increase in movie ticket prices. Other methods employed to reduce upward bias resulting from a sharp rise in one item or component are geometric and harmonic averages. A comparison of all these procedures for the hypothetical consumer is shown in Table II, and selected indexes are graphed in Chart IV.

20

For comparison, another type of index number construction which might be used is the simple aggregative type. For the consumer under discussion, the total of the prices of the items he buys in the base period is $2,165.95. In year 2, the total of these prices is $2,381.22. A simple aggregative index number for year 2 is

$$I_{1\,2}=\Sigma p_2/\Sigma p_1=109.9.$$

This procedure implicitly gives the highest weight to the item which has the largest price change in absolute terms. In year 2 that item is automobiles which increased $200. This index is thus highly dependent upon the units for which prices are quoted. Simple aggregative indexes are given for the four years in Table II and in Chart IV. The chart illustrates that this index has practically no increase in the fourth year when auto prices do not rise while the other indexes shown continue to climb.

Both of these simple index methods raise questions of how to reduce biases in price indexes which arise due to large relative

Chart IV

COMPARISON OF SELECTED SIMPLE AND WEIGHTED PRICE INDEXES FOR HYPOTHETICAL CONSUMER

YEAR 1 = 100

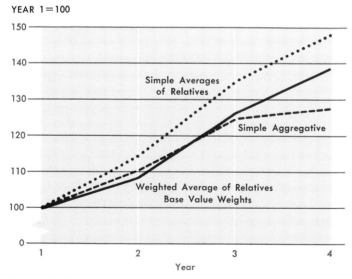

Source: Table I.

21

price changes (the movie ticket example) or large absolute price changes which may be small relative to the price of the item (the automobile example). While both of the simple indexes appear to be unweighted, they actually contain implicit weights, due to either actual price changes or relative price changes. In this illustration, neither of the implicit weights is the desired one. Some procedure for explicitly weighting the items according to their relative importance in the consumer's total budget is needed in order to get a valid indication of the true impact of price changes upon the consumer.

CHOICE OF WEIGHTS The kinds of weights needed to correct the bias resulting from the simple index methods are obvious. An indication of the relative importance of individual items in the consumer's budget can be obtained from the quantities he purchases. It is known, of course, that consumers change the mix of their purchases in response to changes in prices, depending upon whether individual items are necessities or luxuries. Business purchasers presumably do the same to the extent that substitution of items is possible. A difficult question to resolve, therefore, is what quantities to use as weights.

For example, in Table I, the consumer's total budget or expenditure in year 1 was $3,357.50 (i.e., $\Sigma p_1 q_1$). His total expenditure in year 2 was $3,666.50 (i.e., $\Sigma p_2 q_2$). A ratio of these expenditures would not result in a valid price index under most circumstances. Since quantities change as well as prices, the resulting ratio is not a pure index of price changes, but simply a ratio of budgets or total expenditures. The consumer's standard of living may have changed at the same time as a result of changes in his income, changes in the quality of items which he purchased, and for numerous other reasons. One type of question which a price index is commonly expected to answer is how much it would cost the consumer in the current period to purchase exactly the same mix of items ("market basket") that he purchased in the base period, assuming no change in the quality and utility of the goods and services he selected. The latter assumption is difficult to allow for in the construction of indexes, but the desired answer to the question is at least approximated if the quantities purchased in the base period are chosen as weights and held constant in computing the index for subse-

Table II

SELECTED PRICE INDEXES FOR THE HYPOTHETICAL CONSUMER

(Prices and Quantities from Table I)

Simple Indexes

Year	Simple Average of Relatives Index	Median of Relatives Index	Geometric Average of Relatives Index	Harmonic Average of Relatives Index	Simple Aggregative Index
1	100.0	100.0	100.0	100.0	100.0
2	114.3	110.0	113.9	113.5	109.9
3	135.4	125.0	134.5	133.7	125.4
4	148.3	158.8	146.2	144.1	127.7

Weighted and Weighted Chained Indexes

Year	Weighted Aggregative Index Laspeyres Type	Weighted Aggregative Index Paasche Type	Weighted Average of Relatives Index Base Value Weights	Weighted Average of Relatives Index Current Value Weights	Fisher's "Ideal" Index	Edgeworth's Index	Weighted Aggregative Laspeyres Type Index Chained
1	100.0	100.0	100.0	100.0	100.0	100.0	100.0
2	109.2	109.1	109.2	109.2	109.1	109.1	109.2
3	126.1	127.3	126.1	127.5	126.7	126.5	126.1
4	139.1	137.4	139.1	139.8	138.2	138.3	158.3

quent periods. If such weights are used, the necessity for periodic updating of the "market basket" is clear. As will be shown in subsequent discussion, however, not all indexes are designed to answer the specific question posed above.

The type of index described above is of both the fixed-weight and fixed-base variety. An argument can also be made for the use of current period weights, which necessitates the changing of weights with each successive period, while retaining the fixed base for purposes of price comparisons. If quantities purchased in the current period are used to weight both current and base period prices, the question which the index answers is changed substantially. This type of index tells how much it currently costs the consumer to obtain a given selection of items in relation to how much it *would have* cost him to obtain the same selection in the base period. This is an important question, of course, but period to period comparisons are somewhat more difficult than with the fixed-weight, fixed-base type.

In either case, the indexes compare an actual quantity with a hypothetical quantity. In the first case, the index compares a hypothetical expenditure (base period quantities at current prices) with an actual expenditure (base period quantities at base period prices) made in the base period. The first of these quantities may not be what the consumer really buys if he shifts his purchases due to the price changes. The second type of index compares an actual expenditure (current period quantities at current period prices) with a hypothetical expenditure (current period quantities at base period prices). The latter of these quantities may not represent what the consumer actually would have bought if current period prices had prevailed in the base period.

WEIGHTED AGGREGATIVE INDEXES—THE LASPEYRES TYPE   The most commonly accepted weighted price index of the fixed-weight and fixed-base type is that developed by Etienne Laspeyres in 1864. For the consumer represented in Table I, this index results in a value for year 2 of

$$I_{1\,2}=\Sigma p_2 q_1/\Sigma p_1 q_1=109.2.$$

The values of this index for the four years are shown in Table II. The index is of the weighted aggregative type since it is the

24

ratio of two expenditures—the numerator being the hypothetical current expenditure, and the denominator being the actual base period expenditure [6, p. 59].

A strict interpretation of the value, 109.2, given above for this consumer is that it would cost him 9.2 percent more to purchase the identical "market basket" in year 2—if he desires to purchase it—than it cost him in the base year. Similarly, the same selections would cost him 39.1 percent more in the fourth year than in the base year, as shown in Table II. This index construction reduces the bias introduced into the simple indexes by the large relative increase in the price of movie tickets or by the large absolute change in the price of automobiles in year 2.

WEIGHTED AGGREGATIVE INDEXES—THE PAASCHE TYPE A weighted index of the second type described above, which uses current period quantities as weights, is the one developed by H. Paasche in 1874. For the consumer in Table I, for year 2, the index number is

$$I_{1\,2}=\Sigma p_2 q_2/\Sigma p_1 q_2=109.1.$$

Other values are shown in Table II. This index, like the Laspeyres, is a ratio of weighted aggregates. But it relates an actual current period expenditure in the numerator to a hypothetical base period expenditure in the denominator [6, p. 59].

The interpretation of the Paasche number for this consumer is that it costs him 9.1 percent more to purchase the "market basket" which he bought in the current period than it would have cost him in the base period. Again, this index reduces the upward bias present in the simple indexes for this consumer. In this illustration, a lack of sufficient variation in the quantities purchased between years 1 and 2 results in the Paasche and Laspeyres index numbers being very close together. For example, if this consumer had reacted to the increase in automobile prices by not buying one in year 2, the Paasche index which is affected by current period quantities would have been 107.9. The Laspeyres index for year 2 would not have been affected by the consumer's decision not to purchase an automobile since only base period quantities are relevant. Thus, the Laspeyres number would have remained 109.2.

An important difference in the kinds of interpretations which may be made of these indexes should be noted. Table II shows the Laspeyres index to be 109.2 in year 2 and 126.1 in year 3. It may be concluded, therefore, that the cost of the "market basket" increased 15.5 percent between years 2 and 3 (i.e., (126.1—109.2)/109.2=.155). The "market basket" which the consumer purchased in the base period would cost him 15.5 percent more in year 3 than it would have in year 2. A similar interpretation of the change in the Paasche index between these two years, however, would be incorrect. Each successive Paasche index number compares the current period "market basket" directly to the base year. The selection actually purchased in year 3 cost the consumer 27.3 percent more than it would have cost in the base year, and the selection actually purchased in year 2 cost 9.1 percent more than it would have cost in the base year. Since the particular selection of commodities being priced changes between years 2 and 3, a direct comparison of the index numbers to measure price changes between the two years would be inappropriate. A difficulty of this type in the interpretation of the GNP Deflator will be discussed in the final part of this article.

LASPEYRES AND PAASCHE COMPARED   Both of the weighted aggregative indexes appear to be superior to any of the previously discussed simple indexes. They reduce the likelihood of misleading movements in the indexes due to large relative changes in prices of items which may be of little importance in the consumer's total budget, or due to large absolute changes which may be small in relation to the price of the item. They are free of the problems associated with the units for which the price is quoted. Aggregation of values or total expenditures is used instead of aggregation of simple prices or price relatives.

There is a considerable body of literature on the Laspeyres and Paasche indexes, and numerous arguments for and against the use of each of them have been advanced. While it is beyond the scope of this article to review all the literature, some of the arguments are particularly pertinent to this discussion, since, as will be shown later, the Laspeyres index is in essence the one used by the Bureau of Labor Statistics in constructing the Consumer Price Index.

If a choice must be made between the Laspeyres and Paasche index numbers, it would seem that on logical grounds the Laspeyres index provides the answer to the question most commonly asked in index number applications, namely, the change in the cost of the base year "market basket." There are certain other arguments, however, affecting the choice between the two approaches—ignoring for the moment any sampling problems which may be involved. It has been argued that the Laspeyres formula has a tendency to overestimate price changes, while the Paasche formula tends to underestimate price changes. The argument is that the hypothetical expenditure, $\Sigma p_2 q_1$, used in the numerator of the Laspeyres index would probably not be the actual expenditure that the consumer would make in year 2 if he were furnished with that amount of money. The sum, $\Sigma p_2 q_1$, would be sufficient to allow the consumer to obtain the base period "market basket," but in a period of generally rising prices, that sum would be larger than the base period expenditure, $\Sigma p_1 q_1$. Thus, the rational consumer would tend to adjust his purchases, including the substitution of some items for those in the original "market basket" to allow him the same standard of living as before without having to duplicate the base period purchases exactly. To the extent that this is true, the measure of price change applicable to the consumer is somewhat overstated by the Laspeyres index.

The Paasche index, on the other hand, contains the hypothetical expenditure, $\Sigma p_1 q_2$, in the denominator for year 2. In a period of generally rising prices this sum is lower than the numerator, $\Sigma p_2 q_2$, which represents the current period's actual expenditure. Thus, the argument is that if the lower sum of money had been given to the consumer in the base period, he probably would have adjusted to a different set of commodities that would have yielded him the highest possible standard of living for that total expenditure rather than necessarily the "market basket" he would choose in year 2 when he has a higher sum available. To the extent that this is true, the measure of price change applicable to the consumer is likely to be understated by the Paasche formula.

These arguments, advanced by Mudgett [17, pp. 34-40], do not necessarily mean that in all cases the two indexes are biased, nor do they imply that the Laspeyres number is necessarily greater than the Paasche, since actual quantities purchased respond to economic factors too numerous to evaluate. It is possible that particular economic circumstances may create biases in the opposite direction from those mentioned above. For example, if consumers shift purchases toward goods or services that are advancing rapidly in price, the use of base period quantity weights in the Laspeyres index may cause it to underestimate actual price changes.

To the extent that biases exist, they cannot be quantified because what the consumer might have done cannot be experimentally observed. These potential weaknesses, however, illustrate why it is frequently argued that neither of the indexes provides a valid measure of changes in the cost of living. A cost of living index should measure the change in the cost of obtaining a given standard of living from one period to another. Living standards are determined subjectively by the consumer, and he does in fact shift his purchases in response to changing prices in order to avoid giving up a customary standard or to obtain a higher one. Therefore, an index which cannot take into consideration such adjustments, and thereby hold constant a given standard of living to measure the change in the cost of obtaining it, cannot be a reliable index of the cost of living.[3]

FISHER'S "IDEAL" AND EDGEWORTH'S INDEXES

Concern about potential biases in the Laspeyres and Paasche indexes led Fisher to develop a number of tests for estimating the magnitude of error in various index number formulas [6, Ch. 11]. The result of these efforts was Fisher's "Ideal" index which recognized the opposing tendencies toward bias in the Laspeyres and Paasche approaches. The "Ideal" index is the geometric average of the Laspeyres and Paasche indexes. A geometric average is the n-th root of the product of n numbers (i.e., the geometric average of two index numbers is the square root of their product), and it always yields a value somewhat lower than a simple arithmetic average. Thus, the "Ideal" index is closer to the lower of the Laspeyres or Paasche results. The values of this index are given for the hypothetical consumer in Table II.

---

[3] The problems of constructing cost of living indexes have resulted in extensive research. For detailed discussion, see Ulmer [21], Frisch [7], and Konus [14].

Due to computational difficulties involved in the practical application of the "Ideal" index to large samples of price data, Edgeworth developed a close approximation which makes use of quantity data for both the base and current periods. Edgeworth's index is defined as

$$I_{1\,2} = \Sigma(q_1 + q_2)p_2 / \Sigma(q_1 + q_2)p_1,$$

where year 1 is the base. For comparison, values of this index for the hypothetical consumer are also shown in Table II [15, Ch. 13].

WEIGHTED AVERAGE OF RELATIVES INDEXES

In terms of conceptual differences, the indexes already discussed essentially cover the field. The weighted average of relatives index number differs not so much in concept as in formula construction —a fact which has important practical value in the calculation of the index. It was noted in the discussion of weighted aggregative indexes that prices are weighted by quantities purchased. By comparison, the weighted average of relatives index weights price relatives (ratios of prices) by total expenditures (values of purchases). A choice must be made again between base period or current period expenditures as the weights. Consider first this type of index using base period expenditures as weights (i.e., base value weights). The index for year 2, where year 1 is the base is

$$I_{1\,2} = \Sigma\left[\frac{p_2}{p_1} \cdot p_1 q_1\right] \Big/ \Sigma p_1 q_1.$$

The price relative is the simple ratio of prices, p_2/p_1. The base value weight is the total expenditure in the base period, $p_1 q_1$, for an individual commodity. The weight is multiplied by the price ratio and these quantities are summed for all items in the "market basket." The denominator is the base period expenditure on all items in the "market basket." It can be seen above that p_1's in the numerator cancel so that the formula reduces algebraically and is identical to the Laspeyres type weighted aggregative index. This is not the important distinction, however, because the formula is used as it is shown rather than in its reduced form. As a practical matter, quantities purchased are seldom readily available which makes the direct application of the Laspeyres formula difficult. But prices of items and actual expenditures on individual items are more readily available, which means that the weighted average of relatives index can be applied more easily than any of the other weighted indexes discussed. With minor modification, this index is the one applied by the Bureau of Labor Statistics in deriving the Consumer Price Index, and, therefore, the result is the same as the Laspeyres method [15, Ch. 13].

It is also possible to construct a weighted average of relatives index with current value weights by substituting current period expenditures, p_2q_2, in the numerator and the total of current period expenditures for the given "market basket," Σp_2q_2, in the denominator. This index does *not* reduce to the Paasche weighted aggregative index, but it is easier to apply than the Paasche index for the same reasons as those given above. This construction is known as the Palgrave index formula. It has received little attention by students of index numbers since Fisher [6, Ch. 3], and is discussed here only for completeness. For comparison, the values of the two weighted average of relatives indexes are given in Table II for the hypothetical consumer, and the index with base value weights is also shown in Chart IV.

CHAIN INDEXES All of the indexes discussed thus far have been fixed-base indexes. That is, it is assumed that the base period upon which the index is computed does not change with each successive period. Chain indexes involve a constantly shifting base period.

The use of a fixed-base index assumes that the span of time between the base period and the current period is sufficiently homogeneous to allow a valid comparison of prices in the current year with those in the base year. It is obvious that this is a difficult assumption to satisfy fully when economic circumstances are rapidly changing and technological progress is occurring which affects the quality of items covered by the index. At best it means that frequent updating of the weights and revision of the sample of commodities in the "market basket" are essential. A fixed-base index with base period weights is particularly suspect in this connection, and this is the concept used in constructing most major price indexes in use today. A fixed-base index using current period weights such as the Paasche type is perhaps less subject to criticism on this score although it is questionable whether such an index gives the most useful measure in the first place. Even so, base period prices are still the basis of comparison. Given that an index of the Laspeyres type is the preferred concept, the problem of how to make it consistently valid over any reasonably long period of time becomes significant.

A fixed-base index with base period weights for any given year is independent of price changes that have occurred in any year between the current one and the base year. Intervening price changes, however, may have significantly affected spending patterns. A chain index is an expedient measure for resolving this difficulty. The procedure entails updating the base one period at a time so that the index for any given period uses the previous period as a base. The indexes are then linked together in a multiplicative fashion. Using the Laspeyres formula as an example,

$$I_{1\,2} = \Sigma p_2 q_1 / \Sigma p_1 q_1,$$
$$I_{2\,3} = \Sigma p_3 q_2 / \Sigma p_2 q_2, \text{ and}$$
$$I_{1\,3} = I_{1\,2} \cdot I_{2\,3}, \text{ etc.}$$

The chain index for year 3 uses the quantities purchased in year 2 as weights. The index for any given year can be expressed with any earlier year as the base by multiplying the indexes starting with that earlier year.

Table II shows values of the chained Laspeyres index, for the hypothetical consumer, using year 1 as the base. Table III gives all combinations of the chained Laspeyres index for the four years.

Table III

CHAINED LASPEYRES INDEX FOR HYPOTHETICAL CONSUMER

(Prices and Quantities from Table I)

$I_{1\,2} = 109.2$	$I_{1\,3} = 126.1$	$I_{1\,4} = 158.3$
	$I_{2\,3} = 115.5$	$I_{2\,4} = 145.1$
		$I_{3\,4} = 125.5$

Price increases occurring between years 3 and 4, as measured by the Laspeyres formula, are larger than in any other two successive years in this illustration. The effect of the chaining procedure is evident in the value of $I_{1\,4}$, which shows the compounded result of the price rises of each successive year. It is also possible that any consistent biases present in the index formula will lead to cumulative error by chaining. The chained Laspeyres index indicates price increases to be 13.8 percent greater between years 1 and 4 than the fixed-base Laspeyres index (i.e., 158.3 vs. 139.1). While the divergence between the two indexes is large in the fourth year, the example does not imply that the chain method is invalid as such.

The use of the chain method has been urged by Mudgett as one means of keeping the index close to the market situation [17, pp. 70-78]. It allows for the shifting of purchases in response to changes in prices more readily than does the fixed-base type. Thus, in a period of rapidly changing prices, such as the current period, the chain method has some attraction, particularly as a supplement to a fixed-base index. The difficulties involved in the interpretation of chain indexes, however, as well as their tendency to magnify successions of sharp price changes pose serious problems. The chain index alone, therefore, is not generally regarded as a satisfactory solution to the problem associated with fixed-base indexes—namely, the need for periodic revisions of the "market basket."

Statistical Problems

There are still a number of statistical problems which remain even after an appropriate index number concept has been selected. This is particularly true of a general-purpose index in which the coverage of items is broad and where the index is used to represent the behavior of prices in general. These are features of the published indexes of wholesale and consumer prices. While there are stated limitations as to the interpretations that may be made from these indexes, their usage has evolved in such a way that they are regarded as broad indicators of price changes.

The remainder of this part of this article serves only to list and explain the nature of the statistical problems involved in the construction of price index numbers. This discussion is not a review of procedures in actual use by those government agencies or others who produce the indexes in current use, but is a more general explanation of the types of problems to be encountered by anyone involved in the construction of price indexes. These problems are related in more detail to the procedures employed in developing the commonly used indexes of wholesale and consumer prices in the final part.

SAMPLING OF ITEMS   It is certainly not feasible to derive a price index for consumers which takes into consideration all goods and services that consumers buy. Nor is it possible to obtain a wholesale index of prices covering all manufactured industrial items, all raw materials, and all farm products. Therefore, an index intended for broad usage must rely on representative samples of items. The design of the sample is thus critically important in determining the quality of the index. Just as there are important differences in spending patterns among urban and rural families, central-city and suburban families, and northern and southern families, there are important differences among individual families within each of these groups. For these reasons there is no single index applicable to all consumers. The Consumer Price Index, for example, which is limited in coverage to those goods and services representative of the budgets of urban wage earners and clerical workers, still covers a diverse group. The selection of the sample of goods and services to be included in the "market basket," therefore, must depend upon a valid survey of spending patterns within the group to which the index is to be applicable.

SAMPLING OVER TIME   Once the coverage of the index as to groups of consumers or industries is defined and the selection of items in the "market basket" is specified, the question remains of how frequently to observe the prices of the items included. It must be decided whether the index is to be published monthly, quarterly, annually, or by some other period. Under theoretically ideal circumstances, a continuous observation of prices would be desired. For obvious reasons, the cost of such a procedure would exceed the practical benefit. A satisfactory compromise on the problem can be reached if periodic samples of prices are used, and if acceptable means of estimating interim prices can

33

be derived for those periods between benchmark samples. For instance, if it is desired that a price index be published monthly, and samples of prices are obtained every three months, previous experience with the "market basket" may provide sufficient information to allow estimation of prices and therefore of the index for the intervening months. Short-term movements in an index obtained on this basis are, of course, subject to error, particularly as underlying economic circumstances change.

SAMPLING OVER GEOGRAPHIC AREAS The commonly used aggregate indexes of prices are published on a national basis. Whether the index is of a special-purpose or general-purpose nature, it is known that its applicability is not the same in all parts of the nation in most cases. Just as general economic conditions vary widely among sub-national regions, price changes may vary widely by area. This is particularly true of indexes of consumer prices which include numerous services and highly processed goods. Items which are essentially the same everywhere, for which highly organized national markets exist, and for which there is little variation in costs of production and delivery are less subject to this problem (e.g., some of the items included in the index of basic commodity prices).

If it is desired that a price index (e.g., of consumer items) be generally applicable to a wide geographic area, an appropriate means of sampling among different places must be derived as well as a weighting scheme for assembling the information into a single index. Even so, some error is inevitable in the application of an index derived on this basis to any particular area. The effect of such error is practically impossible to estimate without constructing separate indexes periodically for the specific area in question. Some indexes, such as the Consumer Price Index, are published on a national basis and by narrower regions such as Standard Metropolitan Statistical Areas. While it is clearly not practical to construct price indexes for every city in the nation, it is possible to vary sample cities on a probability sampling basis and thus provide a means of determining the error involved in the estimate of the national figure. Such a procedure has merit in the sense of providing better national indexes, but it does not eliminate the error involved in applying a national index to a particular location.

QUALITY CHANGES AND CHANGES IN TASTES   One of the most difficult problems to resolve in price index construction is the need to adjust the "market basket" to reflect technological change which affects the quality of goods and services purchased, and to reflect changes in tastes and preferences of buyers. These problems, like the geographic area problem, are more serious in an index which measures consumer prices than in one which measures prices of items at a lower stage of processing or basic commodities. Machinery and equipment, construction costs, and numerous other industrial items, however, also undergo technological and quality change which poses similar problems for indexes of industrial or wholesale prices.

It is obvious that a television set purchased in 1970 is quite a different item from one purchased in 1957. It is a higher quality, more sophisticated piece of equipment. The same is true of many consumer goods and services such as automobiles, airplane trips, and refrigerators, as well as machine tools and trucks used by industry. The prices of many of these items have risen in recent years. Part of the price increase, however, is due to the quality improvement and should somehow be eliminated in measuring the price change associated with the original "market basket." Without actually renewing the "market basket," the only generally satisfactory solution to this problem requires gradually splicing in the new or improved item, while at the same time, gradually removing the old item. This prevents disruption of the continuity of the index which would result from an abrupt substitution of the item in the "market basket." As a practical matter, however, the rapidity of technological progress has made this a major problem in constructing indexes of consumer and industrial prices.

Changes in consumer tastes present the same kind of problem. As such things as garters, bed warmers, and washtubs have declined in the preference scales of consumers, the "market basket" has required updating to include entirely new products such as panty hose, electric blankets, and automatic washers. The same occurs among industrial items such as textile goods where the substitution of synthetic fibers for cotton has taken place due to changes in the preferences of garment producers. This problem coupled with that of quality changes necessitates continuous review of the current validity of the "market basket."

TRANSACTIONS PRICES VS. LIST PRICES   It is a basic requirement of all price indexes that prices used in calculating the index be the actual prices at which transactions are made. Often, however, quoted prices do not change while significant changes occur in prices actually paid. Experience has shown this to be a problem particularly in the measurement of industrial prices. Many prices used in the Wholesale Price Index, for example, are sellers' list prices. Stigler and Kindahl recently contended that these prices bear little resemblance to the prices actually paid on numerous industrial items, with the result that the Wholesale Price Index overstates industrial prices by failing to take cognizance of discounts, special offers, and price shading. Their contention implies that the Wholesale Price Index understates the effect of changing economic conditions upon industrial prices [20]. This is a significant point since the Wholesale Price Index is so closely watched as a barometer of inflation. The Consumer Price Index has not been subject to the same criticism since price observers function like buyers and obtain prices which they know in most instances represent the prices at which the goods and services can be purchased.

SAMPLING ERROR IN INDEXES   Even if all statistical problems are satisfactorily dealt with in the construction of price indexes, some error in the estimate of price levels and changes results. This is a phenomenon of sampling which occurs even under the best of circumstances. An important feature of sampling error, however, is that its magnitude can be estimated, and it generally decreases as the sample size increases. This feature makes it possible to state with some degree of confidence (i.e., at some level of probability) how far the calculated value of the index can be expected to vary on either side of its correct value. Estimates of sampling error are frequently published along with the major indexes. It can be a mistake, however, to interpret estimates of sampling error too literally because sampling design considerations and data problems render all major indexes in current use less than perfect on other grounds.

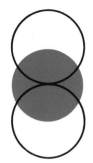

Review of the Major Price Indexes

In view of the problems and criteria discussed in the preceding parts, this final part reviews the methods used by the Bureau of Labor Statistics in the construction of its indexes of consumer and wholesale prices and by the Department of Commerce for the GNP Deflator.

The Consumer Price Index

CHARACTERISTICS AND RECENT REVISIONS This index, with minor modification, is a Laspeyres type weighted aggregative index, which, as shown in the preceding part, is the same as a weighted average of relatives index with base value weights. It is currently published on a 1957-1959 base period. Important revisions have been made in the coverage of the index, however, since the base period. Major revisions were the updating and expansion of the "market basket" in 1964 on the basis of a 1960-1961 expenditure survey, and the inclusion in 1964 and 1966 of additional cities and SMSA's from which price data are obtained. Thus, the modification mentioned above which distinguishes the Consumer Price Index from a strict Laspeyres type is that weights introduced in 1964 are used rather than those of the 1957-1959 period. This means that recent values of the index are likely to be more valid than if the actual base period weights were used, but the index remains subject to the same criticisms that apply to base-weighted indexes because earlier than current period weights are used.

The Bureau of Labor Statistics defines the Consumer Price Index as applicable only to urban wage earners and clerical workers. Its purpose is, as it has been since the inception of the index in 1917, to permit the measurement of changes in the real

37

income of workers. The Bureau's disclaimers of any further applicability of the index have not deterred its users from applying it to broader segments of the population—principally due to the lack of a good alternative index of general consumer price levels [5, Ch. 1].

One effect of the 1964 revisions was to increase the number of items covered to about 400, and the number of cities in which prices are observed to 56. The particular goods and services covered changed in considerable detail, determined by what the 1960-1961 survey revealed that consumers in the defined group principally purchased. This information determined the base quantity weights (q_1's), but base prices (p_1's) were updated to 1964 to obtain the 1964 expenditure (value) weights. (See formula for the weighted average of relatives index in the preceding part.) Price relatives are current year prices divided by 1957-1959 average prices. Thus, the base for the index contains a mixture of information stretching from 1957 to 1964. For example, the 1970 index is:

$$I_{70/57\text{-}59} = \frac{\sum \left[\dfrac{p_{70}}{p_{57\text{-}59}} \cdot p_{64} q_{60\text{-}61} \right]}{\sum \left[p_{64} q_{60\text{-}61} \right]} \cdot$$

Table IV shows the relative importance—or relative weights—of the major component groups in the Consumer Price Index before and after the 1964 revision of weights based upon the 1960-1961 expenditure survey. Weights used prior to the 1964 revision were introduced in 1952 and were based upon a 1950 expenditure survey [10].

The inclusion of additional cities substantially broadened the coverage of the index also. The samples of cities are stratified by size, and data collected in the sample cities of a given size class are used to estimate the index for all cities of that size stratum. Indexes are published regularly for 23 of the 56 cities and provide measures of price changes for those particular cities. They do not permit valid intercity comparisons of price changes or living costs, however, because there is no standardized cross-sectional base upon which to make the comparisons. For example, the average all-items Consumer Price Index for Boston for 1969 was 131.8, while for Milwaukee it was 123.6. This indicates only that the price of the "market basket" rose 31.8 percent in Boston since 1957-1959, and 23.6 percent in Milwaukee. It does not indicate that the "market basket" is 6.6 percent higher in Boston than in Milwaukee, as a comparison of the two figures might suggest, since prices in the base period in the two places were not necessarily the same.

SAMPLING AND SAMPLING ERROR   At the time of the 1964 revisions, some improvements were made in techniques. Probability sampling was introduced with probability weights determined by the expenditure survey. Thus, some items are observed frequently (monthly) in every location; some are taken less frequently (quarterly) in every location; some are observed frequently in selected locations only; and some are observed less frequently in selected locations only. Food items are among the most frequently sampled, and monthly sampling is the general rule in the five largest metropolitan areas.

Specifically, the Bureau developed 52 major expenditure classes into which all consumer outlays can be allocated. It is intended that the weights of the major classes will remain unchanged until the next general revision by the BLS, based upon another expenditure survey. Account can be taken of shifts in consumer spending patterns, however, by varying the weights

Table IV

RELATIVE WEIGHTS OF MAJOR CONSUMER PRICE INDEX COMPONENTS BEFORE AND AFTER 1964 REVISIONS

	Before		After	
Food	28.2		22.4	
Housing	30.7		33.2	
Apparel and upkeep	10.6		10.6	
Transportation	11.6		13.9	
Health and Recreation	18.1		19.5	
Medical care		5.9		5.7
Personal care		2.3		2.8
Reading and recreation		5.6		5.9
Other goods and services		4.3		5.1
Miscellaneous services	0.8		0.4	
All Items	100.0		100.0	

39

of individual items within each major class. A probability sampling method, with probabilities equivalent to individual item weights, then assures that the selection of items chosen to represent each major class will be approximately representative of that class.[4] Also, within each area, the selection of outlets is handled on a probability sampling basis. According to the Bureau, the new methodology permits more flexibility in dealing with such problems as quality changes and changes in consumer tastes.

In addition to changes in methods of item selection, the BLS introduced the procedure of replicated (repeated) sampling in an effort to provide better estimates of sampling error. Estimates of the standard errors of changes in major components of the Consumer Price Index have been published monthly by the BLS since January, 1967. Research by Wilkerson [24] concluded that the estimates are reasonable approximations of the sampling error in the index, and showed that changes in the published index— either monthly, quarterly, or for longer periods—greater than 0.2 percent are significant changes at the .05 probability level.[5]

For example, if the value of the index were 130.0, the index would have to move as high as 130.3 or as low as 129.7, after rounding to one decimal place, for the change to be regarded as significant for the given period. Smaller changes have a high likelihood of resulting from random fluctuations in the sample of data rather than reflecting any actual change in the level of prices. The implication of this conclusion is that frequently, published changes in the indexes which are not statistically significant are given an unwarranted degree of importance by analysts searching for indications of change in economic conditions. If short-period changes which are not significant are blown up to obtain annual rates of change, the likelihood of misleading inferences is considerably increased.

THE QUALITY ADJUSTMENT PROBLEM   The problem of revising indexes to reflect quality changes in goods and services is a serious one with the Consumer Price Index, as mentioned earlier. This problem has probably generated more dis-

---

[4] For details of the classification, see [10, 12].

[5] For detailed discussion of the sampling error estimates and the replicated sampling procedure, see [24].

cussion in the literature on consumer prices than any other statistical issue [4, 18]. There is no entirely satisfactory solution to the problem in a base-weighted index because the "market basket" must be kept reasonably intact to provide stable comparison. Therefore, a dilemma results since the base-weighted index is superior in concept to the alternatives.

The revised Consumer Price Index has achieved a partial solution to this problem and represents a substantial improvement over the indexes published prior to the 1964 revision. The Bureau handles the problem by observing the prices of both the old and the new item when both are available in the market at the same time. The difference in market prices in such cases is assumed to be a measure of the quality difference, and that amount is adjusted out of the price of the new item from that point on, or until the "market basket" is revised. With many goods and services, however, both the old and the new (or the old and the improved) are not available at the same time in the market. In such cases, an attempt is made to determine the difference in manufacturers' costs. This difference is then considered a measure of the quality change and is adjusted out of the new price. There are still some items, particularly in the services area, where these procedures are difficult or impossible to implement, and considerable judgment has to be employed [12].

Although progress has been made, the quality problem is not solved, and to the extent that it remains, the base-weighted Consumer Price Index is likely to continue to give an upward bias in measuring levels and changes in consumer prices during periods of rapid technological progress.[6]

THE SEASONAL ADJUSTMENT PROBLEM   The need for seasonally adjusted series for the Consumer Price Index and its components was recognized by the BLS to eliminate erroneous inferences which can be drawn from short-term changes in unadjusted figures. Seasonally adjusted indexes were first published on a regular basis by the Bureau in 1966, and are published only for selected components which have been determined to have significant patterns of seasonal variation. Studies have shown that most of the seasonal variation is in prices of food, apparel,

---

[6] For a theoretical discussion of the problem of measuring quality changes, see [8].

and private transportation, and that the all-items index is affected only slightly by seasonal movement. Therefore, the Bureau does not publish the all-items index in seasonally adjusted form. Also, the services component which has grown in importance in consumer spending and in the index shows no significant seasonal pattern [11].

Seasonal factors, which may be used to adjust the series, were made available beginning with 1953. While the seasonal factors are produced for the all-items index and for those components having significant seasonal variation, the Bureau does not publish factors for all components. There has been some reluctance on the part of the Bureau to publish either seasonally adjusted indexes or seasonal factors because of the possibility of confusion resulting from divergent movements in the unadjusted and adjusted series. Demand for the adjustments, however, has tended to outweigh the reluctance. The methodology developed by the BLS for seasonal adjustments—the BLS Seasonal Factor Method—is now generally available so that comparable factors can be computed for those series for which no factors or adjusted series are published. The method employed is the traditional ratio-to-moving-average procedure with considerable refinement, and with a means for continuously adjusting the seasonal factors for changes in the underlying seasonal pattern [19].

The Wholesale Price Index

CHARACTERISTICS   The oldest continuously published index of prices is the Wholesale Price Index which is a Laspeyres weighted aggregative type with slight modification. The index, currently published in a 1957-1959 base, covers over 2,300 commodities. Its purpose is to measure levels and changes in prices of items at the level of their first important commercial transaction. To a large extent, therefore, the name of the index is a misnomer, since it does not attempt to measure prices received by wholesale establishments or jobbers. Inter-establishment transfers of goods within firms and goods sold at retail by producers or producer-owned establishments are excluded from the index. The 22 Basic Commodity Index, usually regarded as a supplement to the Wholesale Price Index, represents an attempt to measure price change at an even earlier stage for selected sensitive commodities. This index was discussed in the first part of this article.

The Wholesale Price Index uses base value weights for a period later than the 1957-1959 base, which makes it a modified Laspeyres index just as the Consumer Price Index is. Weights used are expenditures for items measured by net value of shipments of producers in particular industries and sectors. Currently, weights are based upon the 1963 censuses of manufactures and mineral industries, as well as certain other data provided by the Department of Agriculture, Bureau of Fisheries, and Bureau of Mines.

A revision was made in 1967 to incorporate the 1963 census figures on net value of shipments. Prices were updated from 1963 to December, 1966, however, in order that the expenditure weights would reflect the most current prices at the time of the index revision. Base prices are averages of the 1957-1959 period. For example, the 1970 index is:

$$I_{70/57\text{-}59} = \frac{\sum \left[\dfrac{p_{70}}{p_{57\text{-}59}} \cdot p_{66}q_{63} \right]}{\sum \left[p_{66}q_{63} \right]}.$$

The construction of the base for the Wholesale Price Index is, therefore, not as complex as for the Consumer Price Index. The current policy of the Bureau of Labor Statistics is to revise the base weights every five years in coordination with the Bureau of Census timing of new censuses of manufacturing and mining.[7]

In addition to the aggregate all-commodities index, component indexes are published by stage of processing, by durability of product, and by industry groups and subgroups. In the stage of processing category, separate indexes are constructed for crude materials, intermediate materials, consumer finished goods (at the wholesale level), and producer finished goods. These indexes permit some indication of the stages of production at which major price changes occur. The durability of product breakdown allows a comparison of price changes in durable goods industries with nondurable goods industries. In-

---

[7] For complete descriptions of methods and recent revisions, see [2, 22].

dustry and industry subgroup indexes carry this breakdown further and permit comparisons of price movements among industries in considerable detail. Since prices are obtained throughout given industries or sectors, there is no relevant geographic dimension to the Wholesale Price Index as there is for the indexes of consumer prices.

Table V shows the relative weights of items included in the Wholesale Price Index by industry and by stage of processing. As explained above, these weights are based upon net value of shipments reported in the 1963 censuses. Detailed relative weights are available by individual item from the BLS [23].

Due to their lower stage of processing, many of the commodities covered by the Wholesale Price Index are not affected as acutely by quality change as consumer goods and services are. It is true that industrial goods, machinery, and numerous producer finished items are subject to technological change and quality improvement. However, since the index does not cover services and since the goods included are priced before costs of final stages of processing and handling are added, the price changes associated with quality improvements are somewhat easier to measure. Therefore, even though the Wholesale Price Index is weighted with earlier year quantities, some of the tendencies toward upward bias in base-weighted indexes, which can arise from failure to completely exclude the effect of quality changes, may not be as serious in this index.

Current prices used in the Wholesale Price Index have been subject to considerable criticism. Current prices are monthly prices obtained by mail questionnaire from representative manufacturers. Since January, 1967, the prices used for most commodities are those in effect on the Tuesday of the week in which the 13th of the month falls, except in cases for which more representative trading days are known. The Bureau attempts to get transactions prices, but in many cases the prices obtained are list or spot prices quoted by manufacturers or trade associations rather than contract prices at which commodities are actually traded. This problem was discussed in the second part of this article as one of the statistical problems to be faced in construction of aggregate indexes. The difference between published and contract prices is significant in many important industrial sectors according to Stigler and Kindahl [20]. They contend that pro-

Table V

RELATIVE IMPORTANCE OF COMMODITIES INCLUDED IN
THE WHOLESALE PRICE INDEX, DECEMBER 1969

BY INDUSTRY

Farm products	10.7	
Processed foods and feeds	16.5	
Textile products and apparel	7.1	
Hides, skins, leather, and related products	1.3	
Fuels and related products, and power	6.8	
Chemicals and allied products	5.9	
Rubber and plastic products	2.4	
Lumber and wood products	2.7	
Pulp, paper, and allied products	4.8	
Metals and metal products	13.4	
Machinery and equipment	12.3	
Furniture and household durables	3.5	
Nonmetallic mineral products	3.1	
Transportation equipment	7.2	
Miscellaneous products	2.5	
Total	100.0	

BY STAGE OF PROCESSING

Crude materials for further processing	11.3	
Foodstuffs and feedstuffs		7.5
Nonfood materials except fuel		2.9
Crude fuel		0.8
Intermediate materials, supplies, and components	44.8	
Materials and components for manufacturing		24.8
Materials and components for construction		9.3
Processed fuels and lubricants		2.6
Containers		1.6
Supplies		6.5
Finished goods (including raw foods and fuel)	43.9	
Consumer goods		33.8
Producer finished goods		10.1
Total	100.0	

ducers delay published reductions of prices longer than published increases. This conclusion implies that in periods of softening economic activity, the Wholesale Price Index may overstate the level of industrial prices.

SEASONAL ADJUSTMENTS AND SAMPLING ERRORS

The BLS does not publish seasonally adjusted values of the Wholesale Price Index or its components. However, it does provide seasonally adjusted monthly percentage changes in the all-commodities index, and in the aggregate indexes for farm products and processed foods and feeds, farm products, processed foods and feeds, and industrial commodities. These figures are published in the Bureau's monthly press releases. Some significant differences occur in the comparison of adjusted and unadjusted percentage changes, particularly when monthly changes are used to calculate annual percentage rates of change. It is possible to obtain seasonally adjusted series for the Wholesale Price Index on a basis roughly comparable to the seasonally adjusted Consumer Price Index by using the Bureau's Seasonal Factor Method.

Estimates of sampling error for the Wholesale Price Index are not produced by the BLS. The sample employed for the index does not lend itself as well to the measurement of sampling error as does the Consumer Price Index sample (i.e., it is selected purposively rather than on a random sampling basis). The number of reporters from whom price information is obtained is very small for many of the individual commodities. The methods of aggregation used—by industry, durability of product, and stage of processing—result in heterogeneous groupings of individual items. While the sample is already very large, an even larger sample would be needed, in view of the diversity of products covered, in order to develop reliable estimates of sampling error.

The Implicit Deflator for GNP

The methodology of the GNP Deflator was discussed in broad terms in the first part of this article. Since the index is not obtained by direct price measurement as the other major indexes are, its values depend upon the indexes already discussed as well as others. The consumer expenditure component of GNP is adjusted for price change—i.e., deflated—by dividing each category of consumer spending by the appropriate index of consumer prices. Business expenditures for capital equipment, raw materials, or semi-finished goods are deflated by the applicable index of wholesale prices. Thus, the Consumer Price Index and the Wholesale Price Index figure prominently in the determination of the Deflator. In addition, other indexes of construction costs, prices paid by farmers, import prices, etc., are used to deflate various components of GNP.

As the composition of gross national product changes, the importance of the individual indexes used to deflate components of GNP also shifts. Components of GNP in any particular period are, in effect, weights for determining the GNP Deflator. For example, if business inventory investment in consumer finished goods increases for a given period while consumer spending tapers, those indexes of wholesale prices applicable to consumer finished goods increase in importance in deriving the GNP Deflator for that period and the importance of indexes of consumer prices declines. Thus, it may be seen that components of GNP function as implicit current period expenditure weights, and the GNP Deflator becomes in essence a Paasche type index.

An example of an individual item helps to illustrate the Deflator concept. Expenditures for steel reinforcing bars are classified under the gross private domestic investment component of GNP. There is a price index for the steel bars which is one of the elements of the Wholesale Price Index. Total expenditures for the steel bars in year 2 can be represented by p_2q_2, where p_2 is the price and q_2 is the quantity purchased. The expenditure is deflated by the price index which is a Laspeyres index, p_2q_1/p_1q_1, where year 1 is the base. (For the individual item, this is equivalent to the price relative, p_2/p_1.) The deflation expresses the expenditure in terms of dollars of the base year,

$$p_2q_2/(p_2/p_1)=p_1q_2.$$

If the current expenditure is divided by the deflated expenditure, an index is obtained,

$$I_{1\,2}=p_2q_2/p_1q_2,$$

which is a Paasche type index, and is an implicit deflator for steel reinforcing bars. Since the illustration deals with a single item, the result is still only equivalent to the original price relative, p_2/p_1, but the concept which is demonstrated here gains meaning when aggregated for all goods and services comprising GNP.

47

The deflated GNP, $\Sigma p_1 q_2$, is obtained by dividing each item or class of items by the appropriate index,

$$\Sigma \left[p_2 q_2 / (p_2 q_1 / p_1 q_1) \right] = \Sigma p_1 q_2.$$

Then, the implicit deflator is the result of the division of current dollar GNP by the deflated amount,

$$I_{1\,2} = \Sigma p_2 q_2 / \Sigma p_1 q_2,$$

which is a Paasche type weighted aggregative index.[8]

Since the individual indexes used to deflate components of GNP are fixed-base indexes with the 1957-1959 base period, the Deflator is stated with a 1958 base. The base period applies only to prices rather than to weights, however, as will be recalled from the discussion of Paasche indexes in the second part of this article.

Analyses of price changes are not as simple with current-weighted indexes as with fixed-weighted ones because continuous shifts in the "market basket" mean that values of the index from one period to the next actually compare different things. Each value of the index is a direct comparison of prices in the given period to the base period, and, therefore, successive values of the index do not provide a consistent series. It has been shown that a fixed-weighted index for GNP could provide better measures of the actual change in prices applicable to the nation's total output, particularly for the purpose of short-term comparisons [1, 25]. This would be valuable in periods such as the present where significant changes in general economic conditions are taking place, causing important shifts in the relative weights of major components of GNP.

Summary of the Indexes

The decade of the 1960's brought substantial improvement in the quality of the Consumer Price Index—improvement of the sample methodology and coverage, measurement of sampling error, and seasonal adjustment. The Wholesale Price Index, while a broader and more generally useful index in gauging

---

[8] For further discussion and additional references regarding the GNP Deflator methodology, see [13].

48

inflationary pressures, apparently needs further improvement in the means of observing price data, as pointed out by Stigler and Kindahl. Some measurement of the sampling error associated with the Wholesale Price Index would also be useful. A fixed-weighted approach to the GNP Deflator is another area which recent research suggests would be worthy of implementation.

Geoffrey H. Moore, Commissioner of Labor Statistics, recently wrote that resources should be put into a monthly index of the general price level which would have the comprehensiveness of the GNP Deflator and the statistical quality of the Consumer Price Index [16]. Also, as Moore and others have pointed out, additional work is needed in the area of supplementary indexes such as indexes of job vacancies and better indexes of compensation per man-hour which would assist the traditional price indexes in the measure of inflationary pressures and changes in economic conditions.

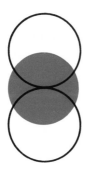

References

[1] "Alternative Measures of Price Change for GNP, 1967-1970," *Survey of Current Business*, U. S. Department of Commerce, Office of Business Economics, Washington, D. C., August, 1970.

[2] *BLS Handbook of Methods for Surveys and Studies*. U. S. Department of Labor, Bureau of Labor Statistics, Washington, D. C., 1966.

[3] *Business Statistics, 1969*. U. S. Department of Commerce, Office of Business Economics, Washington, D. C., 1969. (Supplement to the *Survey of Current Business*).

[4] Clague, Ewan. "Computing the Consumer Price Index," *Challenge*, May, 1962.

[5] *The Consumer Price Index: History and Techniques*. U. S. Department of Labor, Bureau of Labor Statistics, Washington, D. C., 1967.

[6] Fisher, Irving. *The Making of Index Numbers*. Houghton-Mifflin Company, New York, 1922.

[7] Frisch, Ragnar. "Some Basic Principles of Price of Living Measurements," *Econometrica*, October, 1954.

[8] Gavett, Thomas W. "Quality and a Pure Price Index," *Monthly Labor Review*, U. S. Department of Labor, Bureau of Labor Statistics, Washington, D. C., March, 1967.

[9] Gottsegen, Jack J. "Revised Estimates of GNP by Major Industries," *Survey of Current Business*, U. S. Department of Commerce, Office of Business Economics, Washington, D.C., April, 1967.

[10] Green, Gloria P. "Relative Importance of CPI Items," *Monthly Labor Review*, U. S. Department of Labor, Bureau of Labor Statistics, Washington, D. C., November, 1965.

[11] Harper, H. J., and Stallings, C. P. "Seasonally Adjusted CPI Components," *Monthly Labor Review*, U. S. Department of Labor, Bureau of Labor Statistics, August, 1966.

[12] Jaffe, Sidney A. "The Statistical Structure of the Revised CPI," *Monthly Labor Review*, U. S. Department of Labor, Bureau of Labor Statistics, Washington, D. C., August, 1964.

[13] Kipnis, Gregory. "Implicit Price Index," *Inflation and the Price Indexes* (Appendix C), Subcommittee on Economic Statistics, Joint Economic Committee, Washington, D. C., 1966.

[14] Konus, A. A. "The Problem of the True Index of the Cost of Living," *Econometrica,* January, 1939.

[15] Mills, Frederick C. *Statistical Methods.* Third Edition. Henry Holt & Co., New York, 1955.

[16] Moore, Geoffrey H. *The Anatomy of Inflation.* U. S. Department of Labor, Bureau of Labor Statistics, Washington, D.C., 1970. (Report 373).

[17] Mudgett, Bruce D. *Index Numbers.* John Wiley & Sons, Inc., New York, 1951.

[18] Ruggles, Richard. "Measuring the Cost of Quality," *Challenge,* November, 1961.

[19] *Seasonal Factors.* U. S. Department of Labor, Bureau of Labor Statistics, Washington, D.C., 1963. (Bulletin 1366).

[20] Stigler, George J., and Kindahl, James K. *The Behavior of Industrial Prices.* National Bureau of Economic Research, New York, 1970.

[21] Ulmer, M. J. *The Economic Theory Of Cost of Living Index Numbers.* Columbia University Press, New York, 1949.

[22] *Wholesale Prices and Price Indexes.* U. S. Department of Labor, Bureau of Labor Statistics, Washington, D. C., January-February, 1967.

[23] *Wholesale Prices and Price Indexes for January 1970.* U. S. Department of Labor, Bureau of Labor Statistics, Washington, D. C., May, 1970.

[24] Wilkerson, Marvin. "Sampling Error in the Consumer Price Index," *Journal of the American Statistical Association.* September, 1967.

[25] Young, Allan H., and Harkins, Claudia. "Alternative Measures of Price Change for GNP," *Survey of Current Business,* U. S. Department of Commerce, Office of Business Economics, Washingon, D. C., March, 1969.

52

15-401